STATE GUIDES

FLOWERS

Linden McNeilly

Rourke
Educational Media

rourkeeducationalmedia.com

Introduction

Each of the fifty states and the District of Columbia has a special flower to represent them. Some grow wild, while others are carefully planted and tended in public spaces and gardens. Some state flowers are blossoms of fruit trees that will drop off to make way for the fruit. Others are short-lived and die quickly when picked. In 1893, the World's Fair in Chicago planned a National Garland of Flowers, asking each state to contribute a symbolic flower. In many cases, schoolchildren voted for these flowers. Each of them is special and speaks to the spirit of the state that selected it.

Contents

ALABAMA 4
ALASKA 5
ARIZONA...................6
ARKANSAS 7
CALIFORNIA 8
COLORADO 9
CONNECTICUT 10
DELAWARE 11
FLORIDA 12
GEORGIA 13
HAWAII 14
IDAHO 15
ILLINOIS...................16
INDIANA 16
IOWA 17
KANSAS...................18
KENTUCKY 19
LOUISIANA...............20
MAINE 21
MARYLAND 22
MASSACHUSETTS 22
MICHIGAN 23
MINNESOTA 24
MISSISSIPPI 25
MISSOURI 26
MONTANA 26

NEBRASKA 27
NEVADA 28
NEW HAMPSHIRE 29
NEW JERSEY 30
NEW MEXICO 31
NEW YORK 32
NORTH CAROLINA.....32
NORTH DAKOTA 33
OHIO 34
OKLAHOMA 35
OREGON 36
PENNSYLVANIA 36
RHODE ISLAND........37
SOUTH CAROLINA 38
SOUTH DAKOTA 38
TENNESSEE..............39
TEXAS 40
UTAH 41
VERMONT................42
VIRGINIA 43
WASHINGTON..........44
WASHINGTON, D.C. ...45
WEST VIRGINIA 46
WISCONSIN.............46
WYOMING 47
INDEX 48

Alabama

Camellia

The camellia is called "the rose of winter" for its showy likeness to the rose. It grows on a shrub in many colors and shapes.

The goldenrod was the state flower from 1927 to 1959. But women from Butler County said a weed should not be the state flower, so they pushed the legislature to adopt camellias. Since the camellia wasn't a native plant, they added the oak-leaf hydrangea as the state's wildflower.

Scientific Name:	Year Made State Flower:
Camellia japonica	1959

Alaska

Forget-me-not

Alaska has long loved the wild native, true blue alpine forget-me-not. It is a symbol of the wild as it grows in rocky, mountainous places. It was adopted as the Alaska Territory floral emblem in 1917.

The forget-me-not was important to Benny Benson, an Aleut boy who won a contest for designing the Alaskan flag in 1927. He said that the blue background of the flag represented the sky and the forget-me-not. It was officially adopted as the state flower of Alaska in 1959 when it became part of the United States.

Scientific Name:	Year Made State Flower:
Myosotis alpestris	1959

Arizona

Saguaro (giant cactus) blossom

A saguaro is huge—up to fifty feet (15.24 meters) high—with many arm-like limbs that end in white blossoms. The flowers bloom at night, growing in the desert and mountain slopes.

A saguaro (pronounced "sah-wah-roh") can live up to 200 years. It can take up to seventy-five years to develop a side shoot, and is slow to reproduce. This makes the giant saguaro cactus a candidate for the endangered species list.

Scientific Name:	Year Made State Flower:
Carnegia gigantea	1901

Arkansas

Apple blossom

Apple blossoms arrive each spring in light pink, staying until the apples begin to form. This lovely, fragrant blossom fills orchards each year.

Love Barton, a chief advocate of the apple blossom as the choice for state flower, tirelessly promoted it. At the time, 400 varieties of apples were grown in Arkansas. One of the high points of her lobbying was to take a bushel of apples to the Senate chamber in 1901.

Scientific Name:	Year Made State Flower:
Malus domestica	1901

California

California poppy

In springtime, hills are covered with wild poppies. American Indians used this plant for medicinal purposes. Others called it *copa de oro*, which means "cup of gold."

The California poppy adapts to many of the climates in California. In the desert, its large and deep root structure finds nutrients in the soil. Its seeds also lay dormant when there are dry spells. During rainy periods poppies bloom on the hillsides and in deserts alike.

Scientific Name:	Year Made State Flower:
Eschscholzia californica	1903

Colorado

Rocky Mountain columbine (blue columbine)

Columbines grow at all elevations, but they are bluest at elevations over 11,000 feet (3,353 meters). These lovely summer flowers symbolize the blue sky, white snowy peaks, and gold ore of Colorado.

A mountain climber named Edwin James noticed this flower in 1820 on Pike's Peak. Its rich aroma attracts butterflies, bees, and hummingbirds. *Aquila* is the Latin word for eagle, referring to the claw-like spurs at the base of each flower.

Scientific Name:	Year Made State Flower:
Aquilegia caerulea	1899

Connecticut

Mountain laurel

The native mountain laurel brings beauty to the woodlands in June. The fragrant star-shaped white and pink flowers have attracted travelers since early colonial days.

In the early twentieth century, mountain laurel was prized for holiday wreaths, chains, and clusters. Destructive gangs would use force to take it from property owners. Demands for protection led to the Laurel Law in 1917, making it illegal to take laurel from private property. The law was revoked in 1969.

Scientific Name:	Year Made State Flower:
Kalmia latifolia	1907

Delaware

Peach blossom

Each spring, orchards come alive with peach blossoms. The flowers can bloom in several shades from pink to purplish. They also thrive in gardens.

When the peach blossom was chosen, Delaware was known as the Peach State because the state orchards held as many as 800,000 peach trees. Peaches are so loved in Delaware the official state dessert as of 2009 is the peach pie.

Scientific Name:	Year Made State Flower:
Prunus persica	1895

Florida

Orange blossom

Orange groves are everywhere in Florida, so it's only natural the state flower, state fruit, and state drink should all come from oranges. This star-shaped blossom is small and fragrant.

Citrus fruit, especially oranges, are a major part of Florida's economy. Florida produces around half the citrus in the United States, with the vast majority of oranges processed into orange juice.

Scientific Name:	Year Made State Flower:
Citrus sinensis	1909

Georgia

Cherokee rose

Cherokee American Indians spread this flower and used its fruit for food. It's a prickly climbing shrub that blooms twice a year.

Roses grow naturally throughout North America. They can have a rich aroma. They bear edible fruit called rose hips, which have been used in medicines since ancient times. Birds and other animals eat them in the winter.

Scientific Name:	Year Made State Flower:
Rosa laevigata	1916

Hawaii

Yellow hibiscus

Called *pua aloalo*, the yellow hibiscus is a large, showy flower popular in gardens, parks, and public spaces. There are hundreds of varieties of hibiscus in Hawaii.

The yellow hibiscus is also called *maʻo hau hele*. This means "green traveling introduced hibiscus," even though the flowers are yellow. However, as they die, the flowers turn green.

Scientific Name:	Year Made State Flower:
Hibiscus brackenridgei	1988

Idaho

Syringa mock orange

The white flower syringa grows on a shrub at the edges of streams and hills. It was noticed and recorded during the Lewis and Clark Expedition of 1803 – 04. It has a sweet smell.

American Indians used the syringa for many things such as making pipe stems, harpoon shafts, bows, arrows, root-digging sticks, and for fashioning snowshoes. They made soap of the bark and leaves.

Scientific Name:	Year Made State Flower:
Philadelphus lewisii	1931

Illinois

Native violet (sister violet)

Violets beautify the forests, wetlands, and prairies of Illinois in springtime. They are often in hiding but have a deep bluish purple tone.

The flowers are edible and can be covered in sugar and used as cake decorations. Violets produce a second, smaller flower on short stems near the ground. The smaller flower produces most of the seeds.

Scientific Name:	Year Made State Flower:
Violet sororia	1908

Indiana

Peony

You can't miss this big, showy garden flower. The most common is red, and some have several layers of petals. They begin to bloom in late May.

(Indiana continued)

The state flower hasn't always been the peony. It started as the carnation in 1913, and changed to the tulip tree blossom in 1923. The zinnia was chosen in 1931. Finally, in 1957, the government—possibly encouraged by an assembly member who was a professional peony grower—chose the peony.

Scientific Name:	Year Made State Flower:
Paeonia group	1957

Iowa

Wild rose

Native wild roses grow in thickets in the summer. They can be pink or white, with yellow centers, and are more delicate than garden roses. Their fruit is vitamin-rich.

The wild rose was chosen because it was one of the decorations used on the silver service presented to the battleship USS Iowa in 1897. But the majority of the Senate first voted against it. After the Iowa Federation of Women's Clubs chose the wild rose as the official emblem, the next vote approved it.

Scientific Name:	Year Made State Flower:
Rosa suffulta	1897

Kansas

Sunflower

This impressive flower is actually made of more than one thousand tiny flowers clustered together on a common base, surrounded by large yellow petals. It bears delicious seeds.

Sunflowers are incredibly useful. Sunflower oil is the third most common cooking oil, and it can be converted to biofuel. Since sunflowers can endure high levels of soil toxins, they can be used to cleanse soil of lead, arsenic, and radioactive waste.

Scientific Name:	Year Made State Flower:
Helianthus annuus	1903

Kentucky

Goldenrod

Roadsides and clearings are decorated with this golden yellow bush that blooms late. Its flowers are used in herbal medicine and tea. Henry Ford tried to make rubber from its leaves.

Though Kentucky is known as the bluegrass state, goldenrod beat out bluegrass as the state flower. The Kentucky Federation of Women's Clubs argued that goldenrod was the best choice because it grew around the state, and was featured on the flag in 1918.

Scientific Name:	Year Made State Flower:
Solidago canadensis	1926

Louisiana

Southern magnolia

Magnolias grow on large, stately trees common in the South. The trees, which can grow to 125 feet (38 meters), have thick, waxy leaves. The fragrant white flowers are impressive.

Small mammals like squirrels and opossums eat magnolia seeds, as do birds. Many parts of the magnolia tree, like the leaves, fruit, bark, and wood are useful in making medications. The trunks can also be used as a source for wood to make furniture and veneers.

Scientific Name:	Year Made State Flower:
Magnolia grandiflora	1900

Maine

Eastern white pine cone and tassel

This state floral emblem shows the importance of the pine tree to early settlers. Colonists used the pine tree to build homes but only about one-percent of the old growth trees remain.

Botanically, the white pine cone and tassel are not flowers, but a special kind of plant part that makes seeds without flowers. Their cones are male and female. The male cones fall off the tree after pollination. The larger female cones grow and take months or even years to mature.

Scientific Name:	Year Made State Flower:
Pinus strobus	1895

Maryland

Black-Eyed Susan

A relative of the sunflower, this large, bright yellow flower dots the summer landscape of Maryland. It has a chocolate colored center and stands from one to three feet (30.48-91.44cm) tall.

The scientific name for the black-eyed Susan describes it well. *Hirta* means "rough hair" in Latin, an accurate description of the prominent center of the flower.

Scientific Name:	Year Made State Flower:
Rudbeckia hirta	1918

Massachusetts

Mayflower

This small white or pink flower grows along the ground, blooming in spring. It is also called the trailing arbutus and can be found hiding among dry leaves.

(Massachusetts continued)

It took three tries to get Massachusetts to adopt the Mayflower as its state flower, starting in 1893 and continuing until 1918. Mountain laurel and water lilies were also proposed. No one could agree until a majority of the state's schoolchildren voted for the mayflower.

Scientific Name:	Year Made State Flower:
Epigaea repens	1918

Michigan

Apple blossom

Michigan is a key apple grower, so it's only natural that the apple blossom is the state flower. It's delicate, fragrant, and looks like snow in the springtime orchards.

There are about a thousand varieties of apple blossoms cultivated in the United States. It is believed that all of them are related to the crab apple.

Scientific Name:	Year Made State Flower:
Malus domestica	1897

Minnesota

Pink and white lady's slipper

The pink and white lady's slipper is one of North America's most beautiful flowers. A wild orchid that blooms in June, this plant can take up to sixteen years to produce a flower.

Lady slippers can live up to fifty years. Its rarity has given it protection by Minnesota state law. It is illegal to pick the flowers or to uproot or unearth the plants. Lady slippers are listed as threatened and endangered by many states.

Scientific Name:	Year Made State Flower:
Cypripedium reginae	1893

Mississippi

Magnolia

Magnolia trees line streets and fill woodlands in Mississippi, so it is fitting that the elegant magnolia flower, as well as the tree it grows on, both represent the state.

The magnolia is an ancient plant. Fossils of magnolia species have been dated from 20 million to 95 million years ago.

Scientific Name:	Year Made State Flower:
Magnolia	1952

Missouri

White hawthorn blossom

Missouri designated the white hawthorn blossom as its official state flower in 1923. There are more than 75 species of hawthorn in Missouri. They are related to apple, pear, plums, cherries, peaches, and apricots.

Small red fruits follow the blossoms. These fruits, called haws, can be used to make jelly or jam, and remain on the branches after winter begins.

Scientific Name:	Year Made State Flower:
Crataegus group	1923

Montana

Bitterroot

Bitterroot has showy pink blossoms, but its early use by American Indians was its edible root. It blooms in the late spring and is common in the western mountain area.

(Montana continued)

When dried, bitterroot is a lightweight, nutritious addition to a wild-game diet. It was bartered and exchanged at major trading centers: A full sack could buy a horse. When it was ground and seasoned with deer fat and moss, it could be molded into patties to be eaten later.

Scientific Name:	Year Made State Flower:
Lewisia rediviva	1895

Nebraska

Goldenrod

This tiny flower grows abundantly in the fields and prairies, giving a beautiful yellow cast to the landscape. It is closely related to Kentucky's tall goldenrod.

A wagonload of harvested goldenrod waited at the gates of the Nebraska State Fair on September 17, 1895. Each visitor was presented with a sprig, which was to be worn as a boutonniere for "Goldenrod Day."

Scientific Name:	Year Made State Flower:
Solidago gigantea	1895

Nevada

Sagebrush

Sagebrush blooms in late summer, tiny silver-green flowers on a gray-green bush. Sagebrush has a pleasant tangy odor when wet and is useful for fuel or making tea.

Sagebrush is an important winter food for sheep and cattle. American Indians used sagebrush leaves as medicine and weaved mats with sagebrush bark.

Scientific Name:	Year Made State Flower:
Artemisia tridentata	1917

New Hampshire

Purple lilac

Lilacs represent the hardy character of the people of New Hampshire as the bushes can live hundreds of years. Lilacs have a pleasing smell and purple blooms.

Purple lilac emits one of the most powerful fragrances of any plant. Walking near a lilac is enough to be engulfed in its aroma. Purple lilacs are also associated with springtime, young love, and romantic poetry.

Scientific Name:	Year Made State Flower:
Syringa vulgaris	1919

New Jersey

Common meadow violet (sister violet)

This lovely, small purple flower blooms in the spring, living in meadows and open woodlands with plenty of rain.

Ancient Greeks cultivated violets around 500 BCE or earlier. Both the Greeks and the Romans used violets for medicine, a wine called Vinum Violatum, as a sweetener of food, and decorations for festivals.

Scientific Name:	Year Made State Flower:
Violet sororia	1913

New Mexico

Yucca or soap weed flower

This flower grows on a tall stalk from the center of a spiky plant. It appears across the landscape of New Mexico in summertime. Its roots have been used to make soap.

Yuccas have a special pollination system that depends on the yucca moth. It painstakingly transfers the pollen from the stamens of one plant to the stigma of another, and then lays an egg in the flower. As the moth larvae grows, it eats some of the developing seeds.

Scientific Name:	Year Made State Flower:
Yucca glauca	1927

New York

Rose

New York didn't choose a single rose but all wild roses as their state flower. They grow across the state in a variety of colors, blooming in late spring.

In 1890, the education department asked schoolchildren to vote on their favorite flowers. Out of 130 types of flowers, the rose came in second, losing to goldenrod. But when the vote was taken again the following year with just the top two flowers competing, the rose won handily.

Scientific Name:	Year Made State Flower:
Rosa	1891

North Carolina

Flowering dogwood

Blooming in late April, flowering dogwood trees fill the woodlands with pretty white flowers. This small, slender tree is found in many areas of the state.

(North Carolina continued)

The wood of dogwood trees is very hard and durable, so it was excellent for making farm tools, wedges to split rails, and shuttles for spinning mills. Fevers and malaria were treated with dogwood roots and bark, which could also be used as an antiseptic.

Scientific Name:	Year Made State Flower:
Cornus florida	1941

North Dakota

Wild prairie rose

The rose is one of the oldest flowers in North America because it's strong, attractive, and has many varieties. The fruit, called rose hips, can be eaten and is vitamin-rich.

In 1889, the first graduating class of the University of North Dakota chose green and pink, the colors of the wild prairie rose, as their school's official colors. They said that the colors were "suggestive of our green prairies and rosy prospects."

Scientific Name:	Year Made State Flower:
Rosa arkansa	1907

Ohio

Scarlet carnation

The carnation is a cheerful, durable flower with a pleasant fragrance. Its scientific name *dianthus* roughly translates to "flower of love" or "flower of the gods," depending on the source.

The carnation was chosen to honor Ohio native President William McKinley, who often wore a red carnation on his coat, stuck in a buttonhole on the lapel. He was assassinated in 1901.

Scientific Name:	Year Made State Flower:
Dianthus caryophyllus	1904

Oklahoma

Oklahoma rose

The Oklahoma rose is known for its dark, velvety red bloom. It has a strong, sweet, old rose perfume. Some say the red color represents the blood shed during the forced relocation of five American Indian tribes to Oklahoma in the 1800s.

The mistletoe was the state flower from 1893 – 2004. It had long been controversial, since mistletoe is actually a parasite and its flowers are nearly invisible. Mistletoe is now the floral emblem and the Indian blanket the state wildflower.

Scientific Name:	Year Made State Flower:
Rosa odorata	2004

Oregon

Oregon grape

This shrub has dainty yellow flowers in early summer, and dark blue berries for jelly. The bark and roots can be used to make yellow dye and medicine.

Oregon grape is used for many medicinal reasons. One of the most common is treating stomach and digestive trouble, as well as helping cure infections and skin diseases.

Scientific Name:	Year Made State Flower:
Mahonia aquifolium	1899

Pennsylvania

Mountain laurel

This lovely, wild plant is often moved to yards and public places. It is related to the rhododendron. One nickname is "spoonwood," as historically, its wood has been made into spoons.

(Pennsylvania continued)

Mountain laurels' blossom clusters resemble rhododendrons, but their leaves are smaller. Mountain laurel is one of the few broadleaved native plants in the state that keep their leaves during the winter.

Scientific Name:	Year Made State Flower:
Kalmia latifolia	1933

Rhode Island

Early blue violet

This blue violet is a different species from other states' violets. Its attractive purple leaves are distinctive as they color the hillsides and woodlands.

The violet was voted as the state flower by Rhode Island's schoolchildren in 1897, but the flower was not officially adopted by the state until 1968, making Rhode Island the last state to adopt an official state flower.

Scientific Name:	Year Made State Flower:
Viola adunca	1968

South Carolina

Yellow jessamine

This trumpet shaped flower is sweet scented and brightly yellow, calling in spring. The vines wind around trees, fences and thickets.

It was chosen because its color suggests gold, and its appearance after winter is like a lesson on constancy, loyalty, and dedication to the state, according to the South Carolina Legislature. Yellow jessamine is featured on the South Carolina quarter.

Scientific Name:	Year Made State Flower:
Gelsemium sempervirens	1924

South Dakota

Pasque flower

One of the first wildflowers to bloom on the spring prairies, it often emerges through the snow. American Indians used it for medicine, though it is in some ways toxic.

(South Dakota continued)

The pasque flower, being one of the first blooms to come after winter, is so inspiring it is the only state flower to have inspired a motto: "I lead." The Lakota name is *hosi cekpa*, which means "child's navel."

Scientific Name:	Year Made State Flower:
Anemone patens	1903

Tennessee

Iris

Any species of iris is considered the state flower. They grow in woods, meadows, and gardens. Though the varieties are many different colors, purple is the most commonly accepted one.

Though schoolchildren voted for the passionflower in 1919, in 1933 the iris was added by floral groups who preferred it. In 1973, the state legislature decided to end the "war of state flowers." They designated the passionflower the state wildflower, and the iris the state cultivated flower.

Scientific Name:	Year Made State Flower:
Iris germanica	1933

Texas

Texas bluebonnet

This flower with sunbonnet-shaped petals grows wild on the North American prairie, one of the most endangered ecosystems on Earth.

Bluebonnet seeds have a built-in survival mechanism that keeps them from germinating completely during the first season, which helps them stay alive in dry conditions. Growers must use seeds that are scarified, or treated to ignore this aspect of their genetic character.

Scientific Name:	Year Made State Flower:
Lupinus group	1901

Utah

Sego lily

Its bulb-shaped root is sweet and vitamin-rich, and was a popular food with American Indians and early pioneers. It blooms in the summer on the plains and hillsides.

According to historical records, when food was scarce between 1840 and 1851 due to crickets eating the crops, families learned to dig up and eat the root of the sego lily. Because of this use, and the beauty of the flower, the Legislature chose it as the state flower.

Scientific Name:	Year Made State Flower:
Calochortus	1911

Vermont

Red clover

This flower blooms in meadows, farms, and along roads from May to September. It was imported from Europe, and early American settlers used it for tea.

Farmers grow clover for grazing their animals, particularly dairy cows. Honeybees gather nectar from the red flowers. The red clover represents the natural Vermont countryside scenes.

Scientific Name:	Year Made State Flower:
Trifolium pratense	1895

Virginia

Flowering dogwood

This flower blooms in the spring but the plant goes on adding color with its red leaves and berries in the autumn. Its hard wood has been used to make weapons.

This tree was also called the "hound's tree," and the fruit became known as dogberries or houndberries. Some believe the name dogwood came from the fact that a concoction was made from the bark of the dogwood and used to wash dogs.

Scientific Name:	Year Made State Flower:
Cornus florida	1918

Washington

Coast rhododendron

This water-loving large shrub blooms on the coast with showy, colorful flowers shaped like clusters of trumpets. It is an evergreen.

Rhododendrons are known as "King of the shrubs" as they are ideal for planting in the temperate climate of the Pacific Northwest.

Scientific Name:	Year Made State Flower:
Rhododendron macrophyllum	1893

Washington, D.C.

American Beauty rose

Famous for its fragrant crimson blooms, American Beauty has been featured in movies, songs, and on album covers. It is hard to find due to being difficult to grow outdoors.

The American Beauty rose was first called "Madame Ferdinand Jamin" when it was brought to the United States. It was popular but expensive at two dollars a stem in 1886, so it was referred to as the million-dollar rose.

Scientific Name:	Year Made State Flower:
Rosa 'American Beauty'	1925

West Virginia

Rosebay rhododendron (big laurel)

These flowers live in the rugged southeastern mountains along creeks and mountain slopes. Their big blooms of pink and white appear in the summer.

Rosebay rhododendrons can adapt to very cold temperatures by curling, folding down and shutting its greenery. This helps keep the shrub from the damaging dryness of cold air.

Scientific Name:	Year Made State Flower:
Rhododendron maximum	1903

Wisconsin

Wood violet or common blue violet

This petite, delicate flower adds color to the forest floor when it blooms in early summer. It can be blue, white, or white with purple veins.

(Wisconsin continued)

This flower is high in vitamins A and C. The leaves can be added to a raw salad or cooked greens early in the spring instead of vegetables. The flowers are often used in salads nowadays. They can be candied and also used in jellies.

Scientific Name:	Year Made State Flower:
Viola papilionacea	1908

Wyoming

Indian paintbrush

This plant is unusual because it doesn't make all its own food from photosynthesis. Instead, its roots steal food from the roots of other plants, like sagebrush. The castilleja grows in many different kinds of soil and environments.

The high selenium content of Indian paintbrush makes it useful for treating rheumatism. Ojibwe natives made shampoo from Indian paintbrush, relying on the selenium content to make their hair appear shiny and thick.

Scientific Name:	Year Made State Flower:
Castilleja linariifolia	1917

Index

American Beauty rose 45
Apple blossom 7, 23
Bitterroot 26
Black-Eyed Susan 22
California poppy 8
Camellia 4
Cherokee rose 13
Coast rhododendron 44
Common meadow violet 30
Early blue violet 37
Eastern white pine cone and tassel 21
Flowering dogwood 32, 43
Forget-me-not 5
Goldenrod 19, 27
Hawthorn 26
Indian paintbrush 47
Iris 39
Magnolia 20, 25
Mayflower 22
Mountain laurel 10, 36
Native violet (sister violet) 16
Oklahoma rose 35
Orange blossom 12
Oregon grape 36
Pasque flower 38
Peach blossom 11
Peony 16
Pink and white lady's slipper 24
Purple lilac 29
Red clover 42
Rocky Mountain columbine (blue columbine) 9
Rosebay rhododendron (big laurel) 46
Sagebrush 28
Saguaro (giant cactus) blossom 6
Scarlet carnation 34
Sego lily 41
Sunflower 18
Syringa mock orange 15
Texas bluebonnet 40
Wild prairie rose 33
Wild rose 17, 32
Wood violet or common blue violet 46
Yellow hibiscus 14
Yellow jessamine 38
Yucca or soap weed flower 31

© 2018 Rourke Educational Media

All rights reserved. No part of this book may be reproduced or utilized in any form or by any means, electronic or mechanical including photocopying, recording, or by any information storage and retrieval system without permission in writing from the publisher.

www.rourkeeducationalmedia.com

PHOTO CREDITS: Cover: Alabama flower isolated © Svetlana Zhukova; Alaska flower isolated © Slavko Sereda; California flower isolated © Quang Ho; Indianan flower isolated © Lora liu; Missouri flower © Imladris; Inside book: Alabama © Feng Lu; Alaska © Oleksandrum; Arizona © David G Hayes; Arkansas © Matthias-24-2 https://creativecommons.org/licenses/by-sa/3.0/deed.en; California flower © aderrick; Colorado © Susii; Connecticut © Rita Robinson; Delaware © freya-photographer; Florida © Iness_la_luz; Georgia © Florist Kuniko; Hawaii © All a Shutter; Idaho Ian Poellet (User:Werewombat) Wikipedia https://creativecommons.org/licenses/by-sa/3.0/deed.en ; Illinois © James Steakley https://creativecommons.org/licenses/by-sa/3.0/deed.en ; Indiana © xiaorui; Iowa © Maia Hansen; Kansas © SATHIANPONG PHOOKIT; Kentucky © Maia Sue; Louisiana © Volodymyr Nikitenko; Maine © Peter Turner Photography; Maryland © Marek Walica; Massachusetts © Fritzflohrreynolds Wikipedia https://creativecommons.org/licenses/by-sa/3.0/deed.en ; Michigan © © Charles Gibson | Dreamstime.com; Minnesota © EQRoy; Mississippi © Bonnie Taylor Barry; Missouri flower © Imladris; Montana g Frank L Junior; Nebraska © Elliotte Rusty Harold; Nevada © Stan Shebs https://creativecommons.org/licenses/by-sa/3.0/deed.en ; New Hampshire © Haidamac; New Jersey © Irina Kuzmina; New mexico © © Pimmimemom | Dreamstime.com; New York © Qwert1234 https://creativecommons.org/licenses/by-sa/3.0/deed.en ; North carolina © elesi; North Dakota © Photoglitz; Ohio © Mikhail Romanov; Oklahoma rose © © Srki78 | Dreamstime.com; Oregon © Krzysztof Slusarczyk; Rhode Island © Walter Siegmund https://creativecommons.org/licenses/by-sa/3.0/deed.en ; South Carolina © Skyprayer2005; South Dakota © Bildagentur Zoonar GmbH; Tennessee © Kaia92; Texas © Brian Luke; Utah © Kris Wiktor; Vermont © John Pavel | Dreamstime.com; Virginia © High Mountain; Washington © © Richard Mcmillin | Dreamstime.com; Washington D.C. © Ron Javorsky / Alamy Stock Photo; West Virginia © Famartin https://creativecommons.org/licenses/by-sa/4.0/deed.en ; Wisconsin © Hardyplants at English Wikipedia; Wyoming © Brian J Riley

Edited by: Keli Sipperley   Cover and Interior design by: Nicola Stratford   www.nicolastratford.com

Library of Congress PCN Data

FLOWERS / Linden McNeilly
(STATE GUIDES)
 ISBN 978-1-68342-403-1 (hard cover)
 ISBN 978-1-68342-473-4 (soft cover)
 ISBN 978-1-68342-569-4 (e-Book)
Library of Congress Control Number: 2017931409
Rourke Educational Media
Printed in the United States of America, North Mankato, Minnesota